Learn How to Play the Classical Way

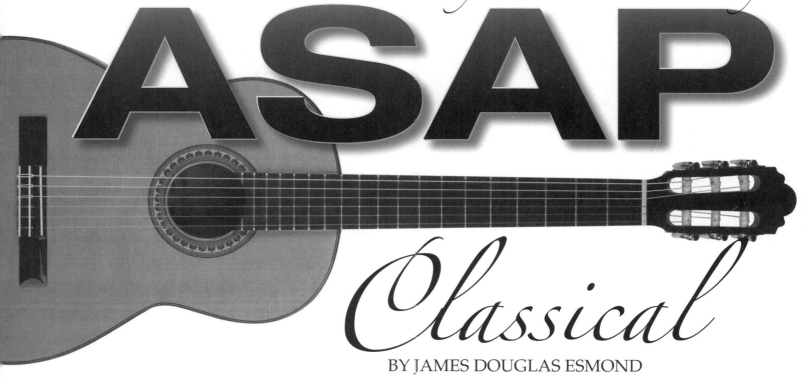

ASAP
Classical

BY JAMES DOUGLAS ESMOND

ISBN: 978-1-57424-237-9
SAN 683-8022

Classical guitar courtesy of "The Music Link" and Ali Fard

Cover by Eric Peterson

Copyright © 2008 CENTERSTREAM Publishing, LLC
P.O. Box 17878 - Anaheim Hills, CA 92817

www.centerstream-usa.com

Table of Contents and C.D. Track List

List of piece playing tips and explanations of exercises

R.H.Exercise Group #1

An easy introduction to the most basic finger patterns used in these pieces as well as good reading for the open strings.

R.H.Exercise Group #2

Moreindex and middle combinations. Start slowly and work for balance in the hand and an even tone.

L.H.Exercise #1

Stay on one string for as long as necessary to get perfect. Moving each finger deliberately and independent of others.

L.H.Exercise #2

Work to keep fingers down until they absolutely need to move.

Spanish Theme

Use this as a reinforcing piece for first position reading by saying notes out loud while playing. Index and Middle throughout for the top line. Work this line separately for awhile before adding the Bassline.

Ode to Joy

This piece, like the last is introduced in two parts and the Bassline will require a bit more attention.

Minuet in C

This piece should be approached like the last two but the parts require even more attention. Follow the left hand fingerings very closely. Get the left hand and the Bassline very good before adding together.

R.H.Exercise Group #3

These arpeggiations will be useful and comprehensive in regards to learning the next pieces in the book. Take one at at a time and practice very slowly.

L.H.Exercise #3

The L.H. and R.H. should be practiced equally in this exercise. Practice the right hand alone and don't go too fast.

Pastoral Theme

Feel the left hand being free even thought the 3rd finger is rooted to the low G. Practice the top line by itself as well.

Gymnopedie #1

This is the first Chordal piece and therefore working on it by "Blocking" the left hand and just practicing the motions that the left hand uses from ms. to ms. will be beneficial. Also practice the Bassline and right hand motions alone.

New World Theme

Approach this piece the same way as the first three "Break-Down" pieces.

Etude in C

For this piece just looking at the tablature and practicing the arpeggio patterns by themselves with no left hand is a good way to start. Then incorporate blocking the left hand motions as well before putting together slowly.

Etude in A minor

Approach this piece the same way as the Etude in C.

Musette

Approach this piece by breaking up the two lines, but pay very close attention to the top line. De-emphasize the Bass notes as much as possible. A light touch when holding down the repeated C and G is good for the other fingers.

Academic Festival Overture

Practice the chords that happen on every other beat to start. Try to de-emphasize the middle voices as well.

A Dance

Get familiar with the repeating Bassline in this piece so it can be put into the background while the top voice and middle voices can focused on more. Follow the fingering strictly.

Simple Lamentation

Practice the Bassline a lot by itself, being careful to shape it and work on having a good volume and even tone.

Soldier's March

Practice the chords without worrying about the rhythm at first and then after working the R.H. motions, combine.

Sunrise

Approach this piece in the same way as Musette, being careful to have a light left hand, especially when moving up the neck.

Reflections

Practice the R.H. arpeggio pattern by itself before learning the L.H. Focus on some of the harder chord changes.

Adagio

Practice the melody by itself a lot to get a very good, even sound. Make sure to de-emphasize the middle voices.

Musetta's Waltz

Use the same approach as with Adagio, take your time to plant the L.H./ R.H. fingers on the ending 8th note run

Cannon

Practice the repeating Bassline first to get it very solid, then work on each 4 measure piece before connecting them.

Eine Kleine Nachtmusic

Special care on the opening octaves should be taken. Be careful not to tense up the right hand on repeated fingerings throughout.

Foreword – How to use the Book

This book, while organized progressively, is constituted of all pieces that are developmental in nature for a beginner's technique. It is therefore recommended but not necessary to go through the book in a stepwise fashion. In addition the pieces can be broken in to several technique categories(i,m studies, arpeggio studies, chordal, etc.) and some pieces fall in to several of these categories. To ease the student into reading on the guitar the pieces have been arrange in very manageable keys, no more than 1# used.

I strongly suggest following all the fingerings that are suggested, however, if there are places in the book where a teacher or student wishes to change a fingering then that should be fine as long as the student adheres to it. There are many options for fingerings on the guitar and the important thing to remember is that the student is building what I like to call a "Technique Memory" and that each piece, or section of a piece can be seen as a set of directions that will, if practiced carefully, be absorbed and adhered readily to the next similar piece. As Guitarists, we are always building towards more difficult pieces but in a way always dealing with some of the same as well so it makes sense to stick closely to fingerings for some time. Write in even more if necessary.

The exercises and 1st section of Broken-Down pieces are meant to really help the student ease into the book. The exercises do not have to be mastered before studying the pieces, especially due to the reading aspect, but should be incorporated into a daily practice routine.

I hope you enjoy the pieces and find this to be fun and helpful on your journey as a Classical guitarist.

Biography

James Douglas Esmond started playing the guitar seriously in his teens. He received his Bachelor's of Music Theory and Classical Guitar performance from Ithaca College, Ithaca, N.Y. Upon graduating he became involved in church music. He has held positions in various churches, as a guitarist, organist, singer and conductor. In addition to his church work, he also teaches Guitar and Piano at Blue Sky Studios in Delmar, N.Y., and writes and arranges compositions in various genres and styles. He currently serves as the Organist/Music Coordinator at Newtonville Methodist Church in Loudonville, N.Y. He resides in Albany N.Y. with his wife Meighan.

R.H. Exercise Group #1
(Right hand Placement, Simple Arpeggiating)

i = index finger
m = middle finger
a = ring finger
p = thumb

6

R.H. Exercise Group #2
(Right Hand repeated note combinations)

- in addition to i/m alternation
  use m/i and m/a as well.

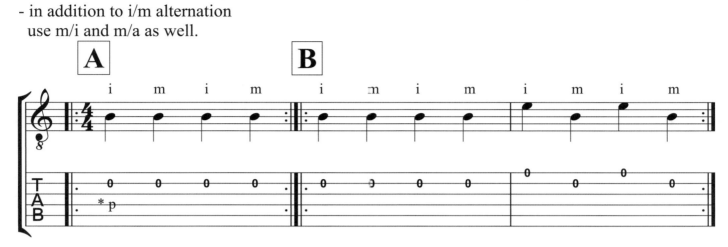

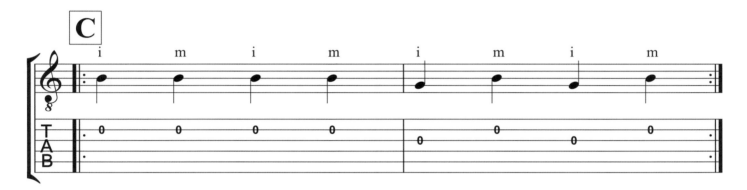

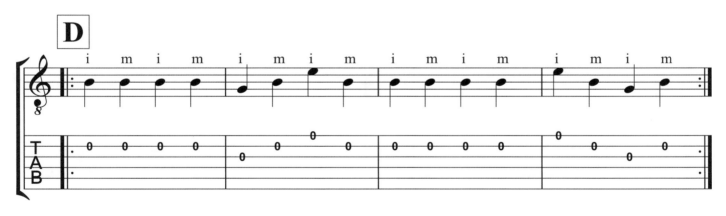

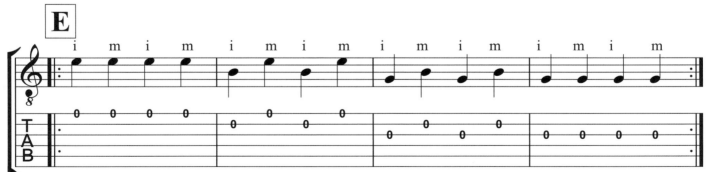

*-Keeping p planted on the 4th throughout the exercise is an option

L.H. Exercise #1
(Finger Independence)

L.H. Exercise #2
(Finger Combinations/Pivoting/Holding fingers down)

(Use same fingering)

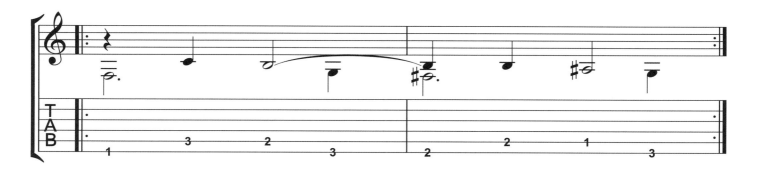

Spanish Theme

Ode to Joy - Pt. 1 (Melody)

Ludwig Van Beethoven
Arr. by J.Douglas Esmond

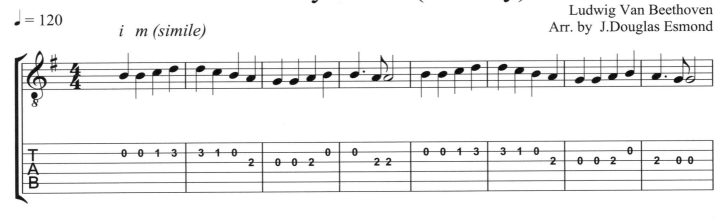

Ode to Joy - Pt. 2 (Bassline)

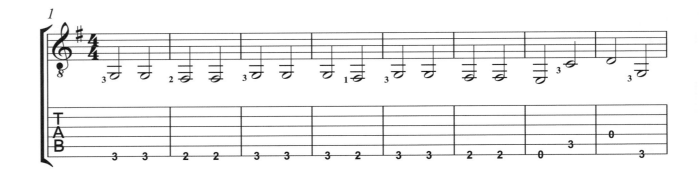

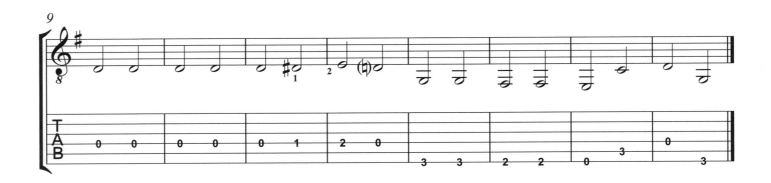

Ode to Joy
(Theme from the 9th Symphony)

Ludwig Van Beethoven
Arr. by J.Douglas Esmond

♩ = 120
Joyously

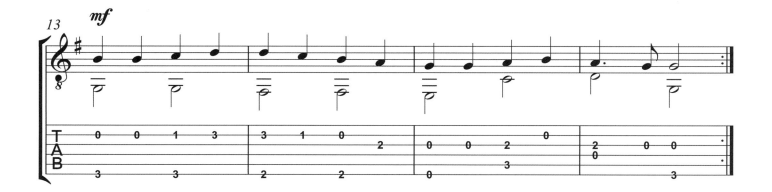

Minuet - Pt.1 (Melody)

Johann.Sebastian Bach
Arr. by J.Douglas Esmond

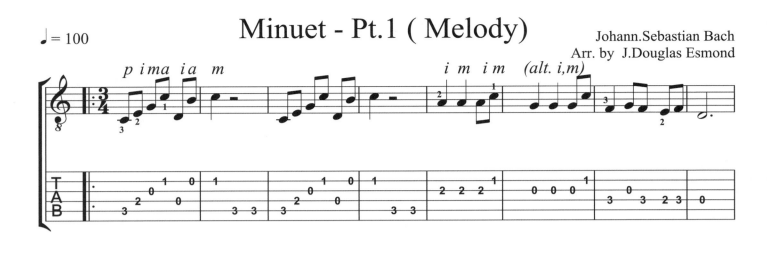

Minuet - Pt.2 (Bass Line)

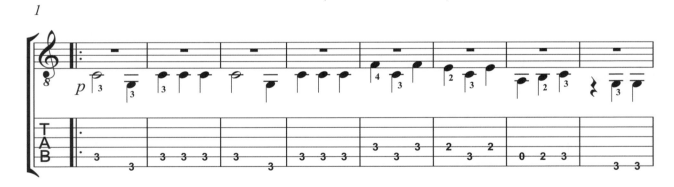

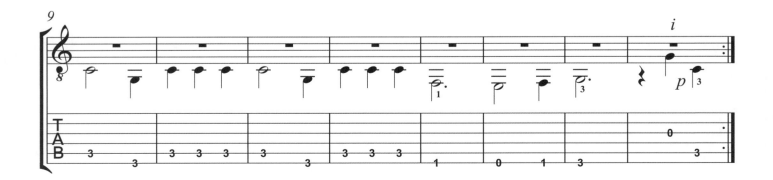

Minuet
(from "Anna Magdalena" Notebook)

Johann.Sebastian Bach
Arr. by J.Douglas Esmond

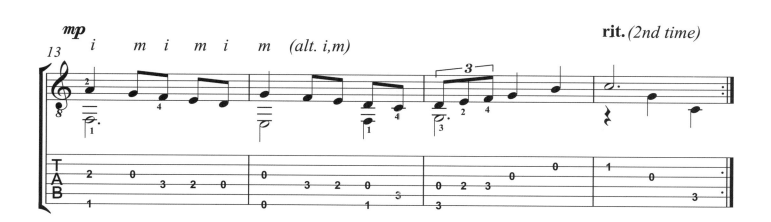

15

R.H. Exercise Group #3
(Intermediate Arpeggiation Exercises)

*(*Exercises can be done sequencially or out of order)*

L.H. Exercise #3
(Finger dexterity)

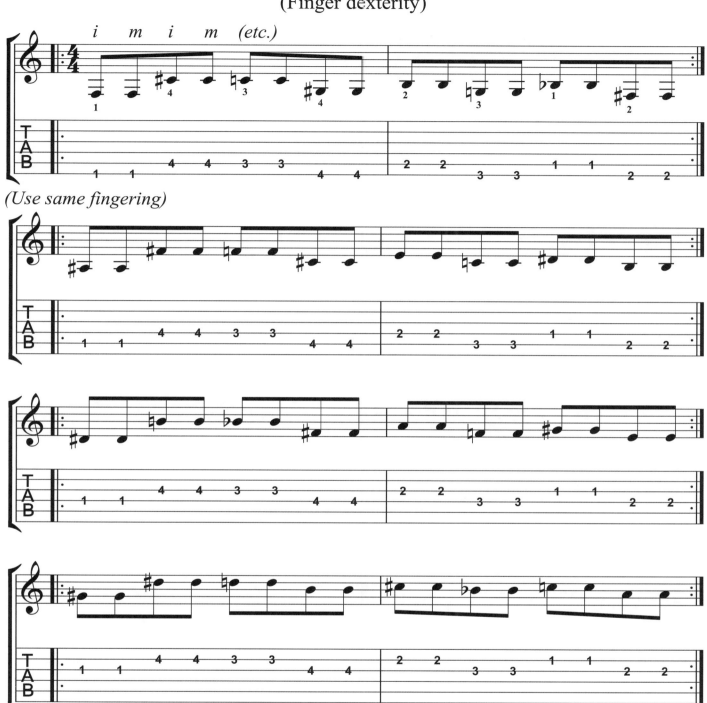

(Use same fingering)

Pastoral Theme
(from 6th Symphony)

Ludwig Van Beethoven
Arr. by J.Douglas Esmond

Gymnopedie #1

♩ = 80
Serenely

Erik Satie
Arr. by J.Douglas Esmond

"New World" Theme
(from 9th Symphony)

Antonin Dvorak
Arr. by J.Douglas Esmond

Etude in C

Fernando Sor,
Arr. by J.Douglas Esmond

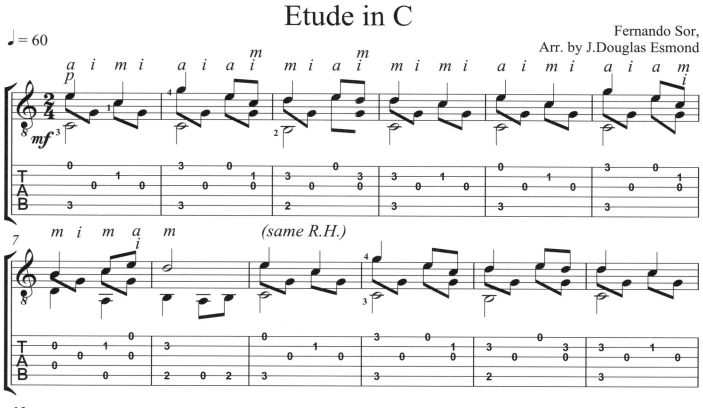

(same R.H.)

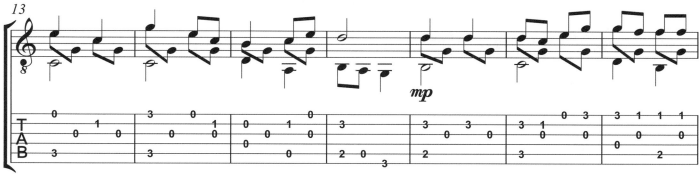

Etude in A minor

Fernando Sor,
Arr. by J.Douglas Esmond

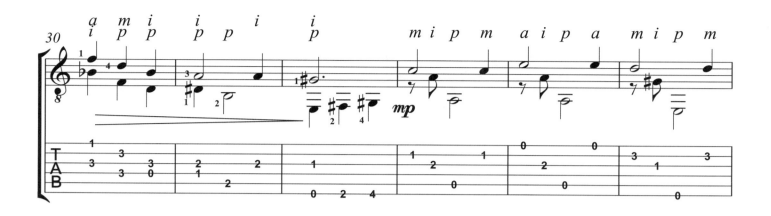

Musette
(from "Anna Magdalena" Notebook)

Johann Sebastian Bach
Arr. by J.Douglas Esmond

Academic Festival Overture
(Theme)

Johannes Brahms
Arr. by J.Douglas Esmond

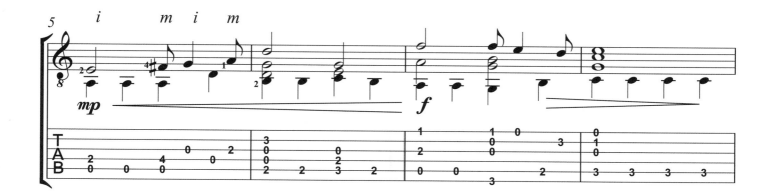

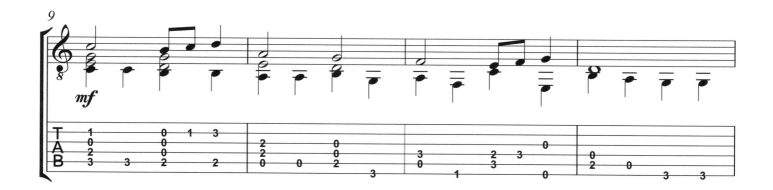

A Dance

J.Douglas Esmond

Simple Lamentation

Soldier's March

Sunrise
(from "Piere Gynt" Suite)

Edvard Grieg
Arr. by J.Douglas Esmond

Reflections

J.Douglas Esmond

Adagio
(Theme from "Pathetique" Sonata)

Ludwig Van Beethoven
Arr. by J.Douglas Esmond

Musetta's Waltz
(Aria from "La Bohem")

Giacomo Puccini
Arr. by J.Douglas Esmond

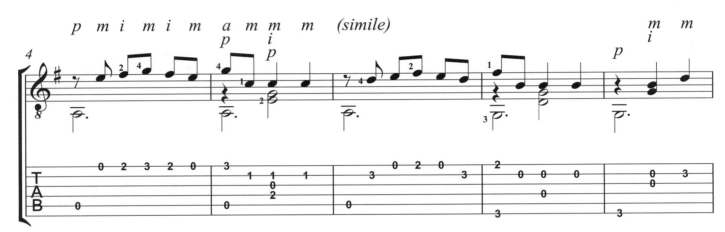

Canon
(based on the "Canon in D")

Eine Kliene Nachtmusic

Wolfgang Amadeus Mozart
Arr. by J. Douglas Esmond

Another Great Guitar Book from the Author...

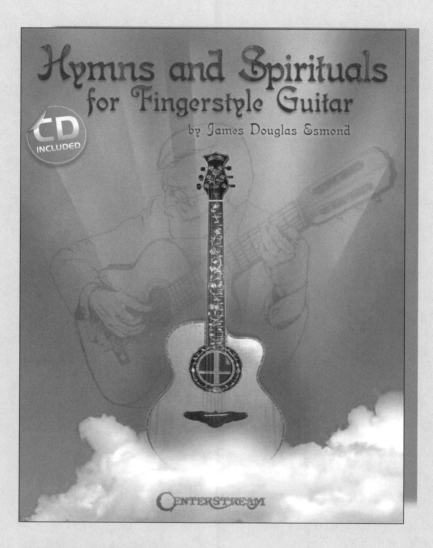

HYMNS AND SPIRITUALS
For Fingerstyle Guitar

by James Douglas Esmond
Originating in the South during the antebellum days, hymns and spirituals are the native folk songs of our own America. This collection features 13 songs, some with two arrangements - one easy, the second more difficult. SOngs include: Were You There? • Steal Away • Amazing Grace • Every Time I Feel the Spirit • Wade in the Water and more!
00001183 Book/CD Pack..$19.95

P.O. Box 17878 - Anaheim Hills, CA 92817
(714) 779-9390   www.centerstream-usa.com

More Great Guitar Books from Centerstream...